The
at M

Montacute House was built in the last decade of the sixteenth century by Sir Edward Phelips, a successful lawyer, who entered Parliament in 1584, became Speaker in 1604, and was later Master of the Rolls. It has long been recognised as one of the most harmonious and best-preserved of Elizabethan houses. Inside the house much of the original decoration, including fine plasterwork and panelling, survives, but the contents have long since been dispersed. In 1931 the house was saved from demolition and presented to the National Trust, who refurnished it with numerous loans, gifts and bequests, among them important tapestries, fine furniture and paintings. As part of the final phase of Montacute's rehabilitation, in 1975 the National Portrait Gallery established the first of its regional partnerships there, placing on loan a large collection of Tudor and Jacobean portraits, which can be seen in the magnificent Long Gallery and adjoining rooms on the top floor. A further stage in the successful collaboration between the National Portrait Gallery and the National Trust came in 1999, when the top floor was redecorated, the environmental conditions for the paintings were improved, and the paintings were re-displayed.

Introduction

Historical portraits seem in some ways to be windows into former times; through them we see the heroes and villains, the kings and courtiers of past centuries, displayed in their finery and presenting their best faces to the world. Portraits are not, however, simple, objective views, and inevitably much of what we see is a reflection of our own concerns, and our own limited knowledge and understanding of the past. This is particularly the case with the oldest English portraits, which are the most remote from us in time, and the most mysterious in content. This intriguing air of mystery will never wholly be dispersed, for we are not able to recapture all the circumstances of history, but even a partial understanding of the context in which these portraits were produced affords us glimpses into the lives of these fascinating figures, the ways they saw themselves and the ways in which they wanted to be seen.

The vast majority of surviving paintings from the Tudor and Jacobean ages in England are portraits. These survivals do not, however, accurately reflect the nature of art production during this period. Many painters were employed mainly on large-scale, decorative, temporary paintings, produced for particular occasions and then disposed of. Among the more permanent art forms, religious paintings, mythological and historical scenes were all relatively popular. However, many religious works were destroyed during the Reformation of the Church in the sixteenth century, in the fear that owning them might lead to idolatry. Those religious pictures that survived the Reformation were largely destroyed by Puritans during the Civil War in the seventeenth century. Portraits on the whole escaped this destruction, and they were produced in increasing numbers as the sixteenth century progressed. Today they dominate our perception of what painters in England were producing during the sixteenth and early seventeenth centuries.

Painted portraits existed in England before the Tudor period, but surviving examples of these early images are very rare, and it seems that ownership of such works was largely confined to the royal family and to a few commoners who had travelled abroad. The Tudor period saw a gradual increase in the ownership of portraits, both in terms of the numbers of portraits people owned and the social classes who became involved in collecting. Political stability and the spread of wealth were factors in this development, as was a growing interest in the importance of the individual. The influence of the Continent, where portraiture was already flourishing, was also very significant. By the end of the sixteenth century it was common for wealthy citizens of all classes to own painted portraits.

The impetus behind the production of the earliest English portraits seems often to have been royal marriage or diplomacy. Royal marriages were organised largely for reasons of political alliance, and the bride and groom might not have the opportunity to meet before the marriage took place. Portraits could be exchanged as part of marriage negotiations, to give the various parties the opportunity to assess one another's appearance. However, appearances in paintings could be deceptive. Henry VIII was shocked to find that Anne of Cleves, his fourth wife, was not at all what he had imagined from Hans Holbein's portrait of her, and Philip II of Spain is said to have 'cursed the painters and envoys when he first beheld Queen Mary'. In a diplomatic context, a portrait of a monarch could be requested and displayed by the ruler of another country as a gesture of political friendship.

Obviously it was in the interests of the sitter to ensure that he or she was portrayed in a way that gave the right impression to the recipient. What was required might not be simple flattery; Hans Holbein's success as a portraitist of Henry VIII was evidently partly a result of the intimidating impression of Henry's power which he managed to convey (Fig. 1).

As ownership of portraits spread throughout the court and beyond, so the uses to which they were put became more diverse. Courtiers might acquire a portrait of the reigning monarch to demonstrate their loyalty to their sovereign; the demand for this type of image led to the production of multiple copies and versions of popular portrait types (see for example, Figs 1, 21 and 22). These could be commissioned from an artist's workshop, where they may have been painted using a pattern based on the original painting or drawing. Artists also probably kept repetitions of particularly popular images in stock. Displays of loyalty like this might not be shown just to the sovereign, but also to his or her most important ministers (Fig. 8). Portraits were also commissioned to commemorate important events, such as a marriage in the family (Fig. 26), or the bestowal of an honour or an appointment (Fig. 12). Versions of these portraits might be produced for other members of the family, friends or supporters.

As portraiture became more widespread and popular, it developed its own conventions and symbolic language; understanding this language helps to cast some light on the reasons for commissioning portraits and the purposes to which they were put. By placing inscriptions, which often give the date of the painting and the age of the sitter, across the background of a picture, the artist destroys the illusion of space, drawing the viewer's attention to the fact that what he sees is not a real person in a real space, but something painted on a flat surface. This tension between the attempt to create a three-dimensional illusion and the destruction of that illusion and reinforcing of the flat, two-dimensional surface of a painting, brought about by the need to convey clear information about the sitter, is characteristic of Tudor and Jacobean portraits. Coats of arms were also often painted on portraits to indicate pride in the family, and as a means of identification. Other, readily recognizable symbols could be worn or held by the sitter: batons to indicate military leadership (Fig. 12), swords to imply the status of a gentleman or a higher rank, rods of office to symbolise particular political appointments (Fig. 8) and badges or medallions of noble orders were almost always included if appropriate. The Order of the Garter was the most important of the orders of knighthood which the sovereign could award as a mark of particular honour; Garter Knights are always shown wearing the medallion of their Order, which depicts St George killing the dragon (Fig. 9).

During the later Elizabethan period a language of symbolism developed in portraiture that was deliberately obscure, challenging the viewer to attempt interpretation. Latin (or English) mottoes were often inscribed on the portraits; at a time when most educated people read Latin, these would have been easily translated, but the specific meaning that they had for the sitter would have been less easy to deduce (Fig. 10). *Impresa*, or pictorial symbols, which also had specific meanings, were often added (Fig. 11). It is tempting to try to unravel these meanings, but this can rarely be done now with any certainty. The use of this kind of symbolism underlines the private purposes to which portraits could be put, as gifts between lovers or friends, sharing private allusions. This culture of symbolism was encouraged at the Elizabethan court by the Queen in her behaviour with her many favourites. These were men with whom she played a game of courtly love, requiring them to profess their devotion to her alone, and to prove it by symbolic gestures.

There were other ways in which portraits were used to convey information about their sitters. By focusing on the meticulous rendering of expensive jewels, or on the imitation of the textures of sumptuous fabrics, artists produced paintings designed to impress the viewer with the sitters' wealth. Women in particular often appear in their portraits almost as mannequins whose main function is the display of costly clothing and accessories. The elaborate fashions of the Tudor and Jacobean period also allowed men the possibility of such ostentation; beautifully engraved and gilded armour, never intended for the battlefield, and doublets and cloaks embroidered with pearls could be shown off to splendid effect. This kind of display had a more important function when associated with portraits of monarchs; Elizabeth I's jewels allude not only to her own wealth but also to the prosperity of her country, and to the success of foreign trade and exploration through which the precious stones were acquired (Fig. 7).

Styles and conventions in English portraiture changed over the course of the Tudor and Jacobean periods, but one constant factor throughout this time was the dominance of foreign artists, particularly from the Netherlands. Hans Holbein the Younger, an artist of German origin, was the earliest foreign artist to make an important impact on English painting, but his successor as King's Painter to Henry VIII was a Netherlandish artist, William Scrots, and from the time of Scrots's appointment onwards, with a few exceptions, painters from the Low Countries dominated the scene. War and religious persecution at home were two important factors in bringing these artists to England; the much greater level of professional competition in their native towns was another. Compared with English artists they were, on the whole, more skilled and sophisticated, better trained and more innovative. They tended to live together in immigrant communities where they established workshops and maintained their traditions of training, often inter-marrying and passing their skills from one generation to another. This dominance by Dutch and Flemish artists caused much resentment among native English painters. However, their own painting benefited from the influx of new ideas and techniques.

Although there are paintings by many of the important artists of the period at Montacute House, the portraits there have been chosen largely for the people they portray, rather than the painters who portrayed them. Famous people, people who made a significant impact on British life, are the priority of the National Portrait Gallery collection, rather than famous artists. Many of the names of the painters who created these images have disappeared over time; during the sixteenth and early seventeenth centuries painting was not, on the whole, an occupation with a very high status, and artists rarely signed their works. The paintings reproduced on the following pages are a representative selection of the portraits at the house, depicting monarchs and statesmen, artists and writers, and occasionally, as exceptions to the rule, lesser-known figures who had the good fortune to be depicted in outstanding works of art (Fig. 26). With their astonishing variety, tantalising symbolism and fascinating histories, they are some of the most remarkable artefacts of an exceptional age, and in Montacute House they have a fitting and beautiful home.

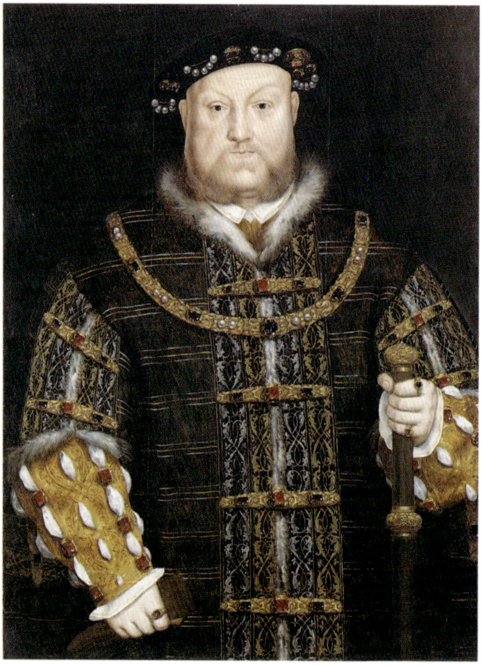

Fig. 1
HENRY VIII
(1491–1547)
Unknown artist after Hans Holbein the Younger, perhaps early seventeenth century after a portrait of *c.*1542
Oil on panel, 889 x 667mm (35 x 26 1/4in)

Remembered today chiefly for his ruthless political tactics, his establishment of the Church of England, and for the fact that he had six wives, Henry VIII was also a great patron of the arts. During his long reign (1509–47) he established a flourishing cultural life at court, rivalling that of his contemporary Francis I of France. Arguably Henry's most important asset in this context was Hans Holbein the Younger (1497 or 8–1543), one of the great artists of Renaissance Europe. Holbein, a native of Augsburg who had been working in Basle, spent two periods of time in England, from 1526 to 1528, and from 1532 until his death in 1543. During his first visit, he worked for the King on large-scale temporary decorative paintings at Greenwich. During his second visit, Henry granted him the title of King's Painter and a large annual salary, and Holbein began to produce the remarkable and compelling portraits of the King which shape our image of Henry to this day.

This painting is a version of a very late portrait, showing the King towards the end of his life. A number of other portraits of this type exist, none of which can be attributed to Holbein himself; it is assumed that the original is lost. In sixteenth-century England there was a lively industry in producing repetitions and versions of Holbein's portraits, often using pattern drawings copied or traced from an original. This painting is nevertheless a powerful portrait of Henry, who was by this time hugely fat and virtually immobile, with an ulcerated leg, but still capable of striking terror into the hearts of friend and foe alike.

Fig. 2
CATHERINE PARR
(1512–48)
Unknown artist, *c.*1545
Oil on panel, 635 x 508mm
(25 x 20in)

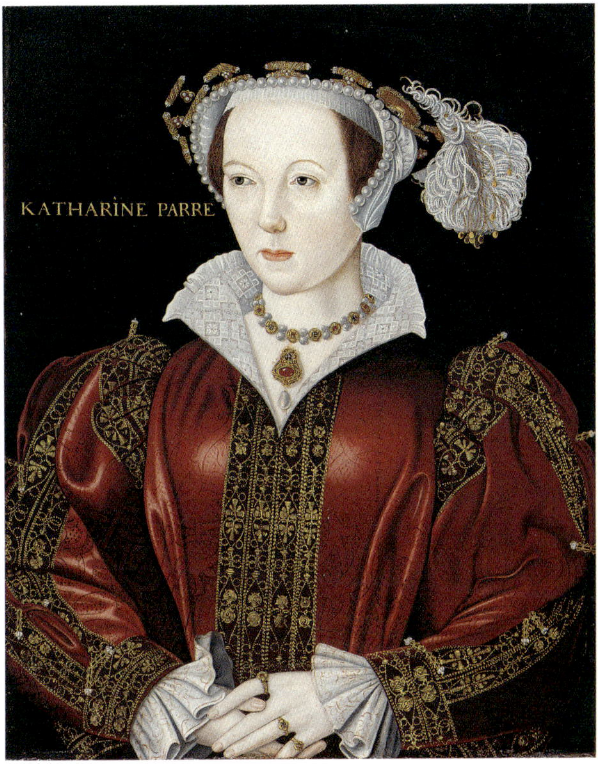

Henry VIII's sixth and last wife, Catherine Parr was set to marry Thomas Seymour as her third husband when she attracted the attention of the King and was required to marry him instead. A learned and pious woman, as Queen she had a moderating influence on Henry, reducing religious persecution and greatly improving the lives of her three step-children, Mary, Elizabeth and Edward. The two Princesses had been declared illegitimate and struck from the line of succession to the throne; they were restored to the succession and brought back to court through Catherine's intercession. She was a patient nurse and intelligent companion to Henry, adroitly side-stepping the plots and intrigues that were part of court life. After the King's death, Catherine was at last able to marry Thomas Seymour, by now Baron Seymour of Sudeley. She died the following year, however, shortly after giving birth to a daughter.

Catherine's pose in this portrait, slightly turned to the left, with her hands folded at her waist, was conventional in portraits of women at this period, implying modesty and piety. However, the emphasis in this painting is on the rich colours and textiles, and on surface decoration, rather than on insights into Catherine's character. Clearly the purpose of this portrait was to convey, above all, the wealth and status of the sitter.

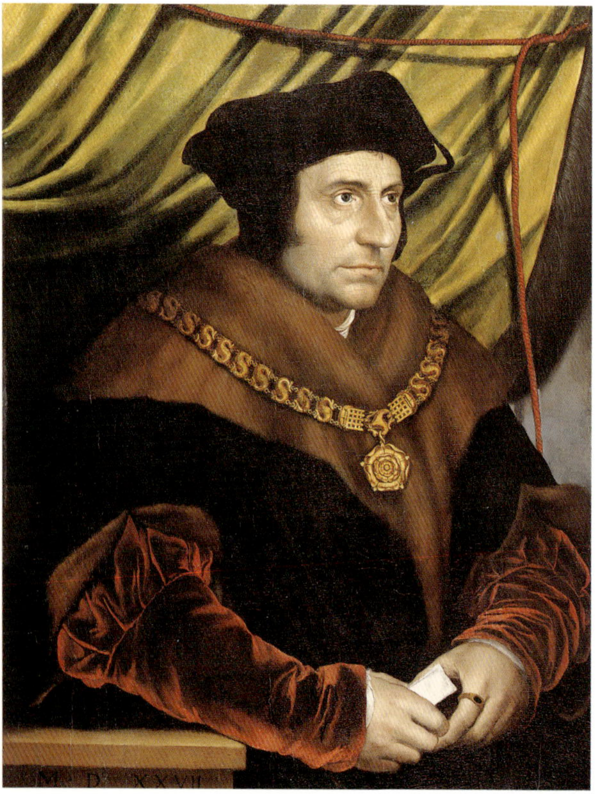

Fig. 3
SIR THOMAS MORE
(1478–1535)
Unknown artist after
Hans Holbein the Younger,
sixteenth century after a
portrait of 1527
Oil on panel, 749 x 584mm
($29\frac{1}{2}$ x 23in)

The great humanist scholar and author of *Utopia*, More became Henry VIII's Lord Chancellor in succession to Cardinal Wolsey in 1529. His close relationship with the King soured, however, when he opposed Henry's divorce from Catherine of Aragon. More refused to take the Oath of Supremacy, which acknowledged Henry VIII as the head of the Church of England, and he was executed for treason in 1535. Four hundred years later, on the anniversary of his death, he was canonised by the Roman Catholic Church.

Thomas More's friendship with the great Dutch scholar Erasmus was an important factor in bringing the painter Hans Holbein the Younger to England in 1526. Erasmus, who knew Holbein in Basle, gave the artist a letter of introduction to More, and it seems likely that Holbein stayed with More's family during his two-year visit. He drew and painted a number of portraits of members of More's family and circle of friends, as well as producing a magnificent single portrait of More himself (now in the Frick Collection in New York). This is an extremely fine, early version of that portrait – in which More is shown wearing a gold chain or 'collar' signifying his high office and loyalty to the King – and succeeds in capturing much of the subtlety and presence of the original.

Fig. 4
SIR WILLIAM PETRE
(1505?–72)
Unknown artist, 1567
Oil on panel, 924 x 711mm
(36 3/8 x 28in)

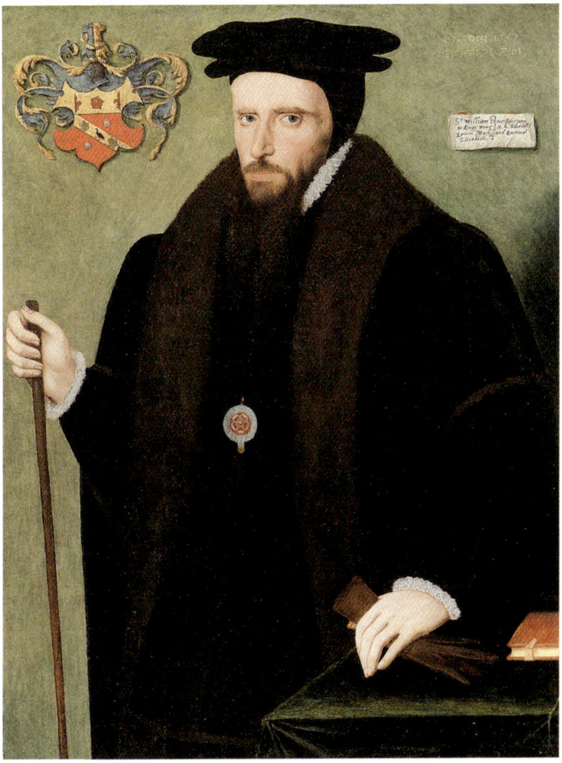

Secretary of State to Henry VIII, Edward VI, Mary I and then Elizabeth I, Sir William Petre acquired enormous properties as a result of the dissolution of the monasteries during Henry VIII's reign. He was granted the lease of the monastic lands at Montacute after the dissolution of the priory there in 1539 and sub-let Montacute to the Phelips family, who eventually built the present house at the end of the sixteenth century.

This portrait, by an unidentified artist, was formerly attributed to the Netherlandish painter Steven van der Meulen. However, the recent discovery of van der Meulen's will proves that he died before 20 January 1564, and so he cannot have painted the portrait, which is dated 1567. The flat green background onto which Petre's shadow is cast, at the right, was rather old-fashioned by this date, but the table, book and gloves were conventional accessories and can be seen in many portraits of this period. The slip of paper inscribed with Petre's name and status, painted to look as though it is stuck to the wall, is known as a *cartellino*. It is not original to the portrait: this particular form of *cartellino* was added to paintings in the collection of John, Lord Lumley (1534?–1609), who owned a large number of portraits, evidently including this one. The coat of arms at top left is a later addition.

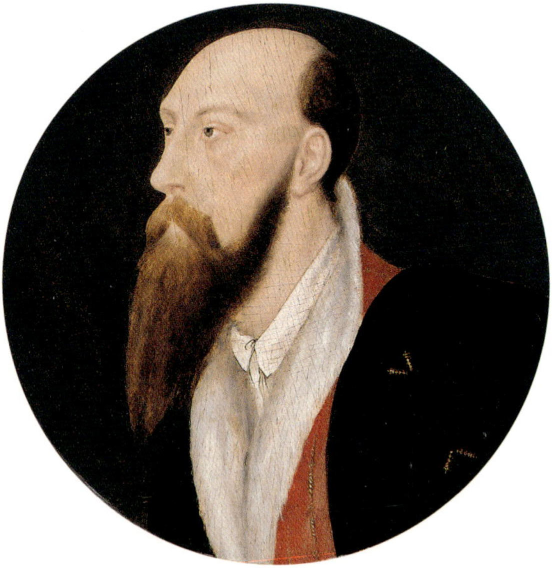

Fig. 5
SIR THOMAS WYATT
THE ELDER
(1503?–42)
Unknown artist after
Hans Holbein the Younger,
sixteenth century after a
portrait of *c.*1540
Oil on panel, diameter 362mm (14¼ in)

Sir Thomas Wyatt was a courtier and poet who, along with Henry Howard, Earl of Surrey, introduced the sonnet form into England from Italy. Among his well-known works is the poem that begins 'They flee from me, that sometime did me seek'. Wyatt had been a lover of Anne Boleyn before her marriage to Henry VIII, and he was temporarily imprisoned in the Tower when she was accused of adultery. He briefly held the lease of the monastic lands at Montacute, a fact that the poet John Leland (*c.*1503–52) refers to in his *Naeniae*, or *Funeral Songs on the Death of the Incomparable Sir Thomas Wyatt*. The Latin verse reads:

> The ancient town we now call Montacute
> Chose Wyatt as its lord and patron; whence
> Its crest expanded. Now its hopes are dashed
> In total ruin. So in Somerset
> Men speak against the cruel fates because
> They suddenly have taken away their Wyatt.
> (Kenneth Muir, *The Life and Letters of Sir Thomas Wyatt*, 1963)

Wyatt died at Clifton Maybank near Montacute, the home of his friend Sir John Horsey, leaving his interest in Montacute to his mistress Elizabeth Darrell.

This portrait, with its unusual circular format, reminiscent of coins and medals, seems to have been based on a lost drawing or painting by Hans Holbein the Younger. Holbein produced a woodcut portrait, also apparently based on the lost image, as the frontispiece to Leland's *Naeniae*. Another, earlier drawing of Wyatt by Holbein survives in the Royal Collection at Windsor.

Fig. 6
EDWARD VI
(1537–53)
Artist in the studio of William Scrots,
*c.*1546
Oil on panel, 473 x 279mm
(18⅝ x 11in)

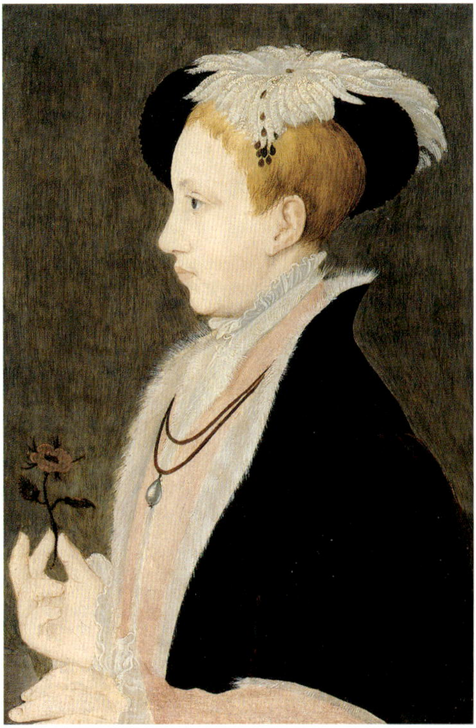

The son of Henry VIII and his beloved third wife, Jane Seymour, Edward came to the throne, at the age of nine on his father's death in 1547. He was able and scholarly, but his reign was dominated by the policies of his two Protectors, firstly Edward Seymour, Duke of Somerset, and, after Somerset's execution, John Dudley, Duke of Northumberland. The reformation of the Church begun by his father was taken to further extremes under Edward, and there was widespread suppression of Catholicism and destruction of religious images including paintings. Edward died of tuberculosis shortly before his sixteenth birthday.

The longed-for male heir to the throne, Edward was the focus of much attention, and his childhood is well documented in portraiture. In this painting, which shows him at about the age of nine, he holds a red rose, symbol of the Tudor dynasty. The picture is unusual in depicting the Prince in profile, and it may be that it was based on one painted by William Scrots (active 1537–53) before Edward became king. The most important painter in Edward's court, Scrots was a Netherlandish artist who had succeeded Holbein in the service of Henry VIII, and who continued to work for his son. He used a comparable portrait of the Prince as the basis for a remarkable painting in distorted perspective, an 'anamorphosis', in the collection of the National Portrait Gallery in London.

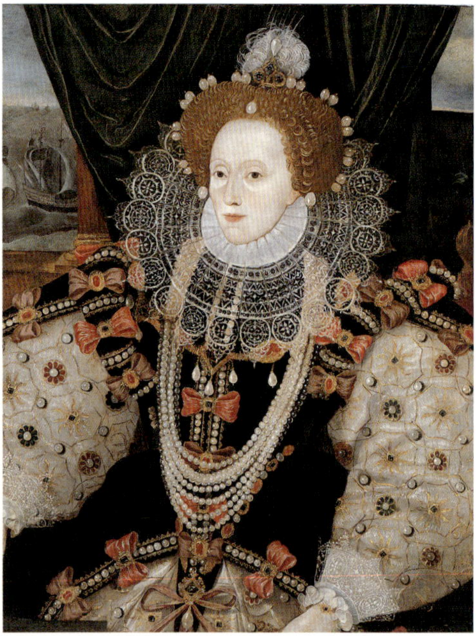

Fig. 7
ELIZABETH I
(1533–1603)
Attributed to George Gower,
*c.*1588
Oil on panel, 978 x 724mm
(38½ x 28½ in)

The great Queen of England who came to the throne at the age of twenty-five and reigned for forty-five years, Elizabeth was the daughter of Henry VIII by his second wife, the doomed Anne Boleyn. After Anne's execution, Elizabeth's early years were hard, for she was declared illegitimate by her father and struck from the line of succession to the throne. Reinstated as an heir to the throne through the influence of Catherine Parr, Elizabeth's difficulties began again in the reign of her half-sister, Mary, when her allegiance to the Protestant Church endangered her life. Her own long reign (1558–1603), characterised by relative peace and prosperity, saw a great increase in exploration and foreign trade, and the firm establishment of the Church of England.

This portrait was painted to commemorate the most famous conflict of Elizabeth's reign, the defeat of the Spanish Armada in 1588. Originally it had a horizontal format, extending much further at the sides, and the scenes behind the Queen showed, at the left, the English fire ships being sent out against the Spanish in the Channel, and, at the right, the Armada being wrecked on rocks off the coast of Scotland or Ireland. Elizabeth's right hand was shown resting on a globe, indicating her dominion of the world, and particularly of the seas and of the Americas. At some point in the past, perhaps because of damage, the painting was cut down on all sides, but other versions indicate what it would have looked like. As in almost all her portraits Elizabeth is shown wearing an elaborate and expensive costume, decorated with enormous pearls, rubies and diamonds, ostentatiously displaying her wealth.

Fig. 8
WILLIAM CECIL,
1ST BARON BURGHLEY
(1520–98)
Unknown artist, 1590s
Oil on canvas, 2230 x 1403mm
(88 1/4 x 55 1/4 in)

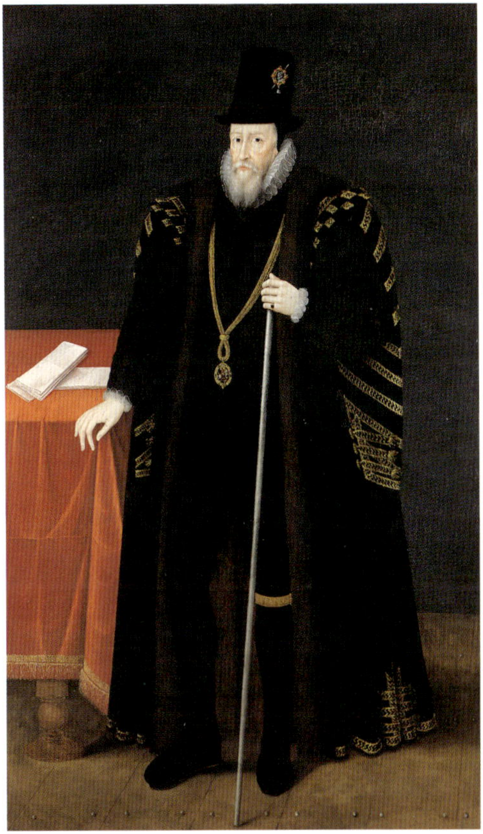

The great statesman Lord Burghley served under both Edward VI and Mary I before Elizabeth I came to the throne, but it is as Elizabeth's most important and influential minister that he is remembered. Her first appointment on becoming Queen was to make Cecil Secretary of State; he was the youngest member of her Council. He was made Baron Burghley in 1571 and appointed Lord High Treasurer in the following year. Cautious but decisive, the greatest threat to his influence over the Queen came from her favourites, notably Robert Dudley, Earl of Leicester (Fig. 9), but he only seriously fell from favour once, when he was used as a scapegoat for the execution of Mary, Queen of Scots. By the time of his death, Burghley was being referred to as *pater patriae*, 'the father of his country', a title usually reserved for kings.

More portraits of Burghley exist now than of any Elizabethan other than the Queen herself. The demand for these portraits would have come largely from courtiers anxious to show loyalty to such a powerful man. However, Burghley does not appear to have been particularly interested in sitting for his portrait, and so most of the many surviving paintings are variants or copies of a very small number of types, painted at different stages of his life. This full-length portrait shows Burghley towards the end of his life, holding the white rod of the Lord High Treasurer. The weight of his responsibilities is indicated not just by the folded documents on the table but also by his care-worn expression. The viewer of the portrait is not allowed to forget on whose behalf Burghley is performing his duties; pinned to his hat is a cameo portrait of Elizabeth.

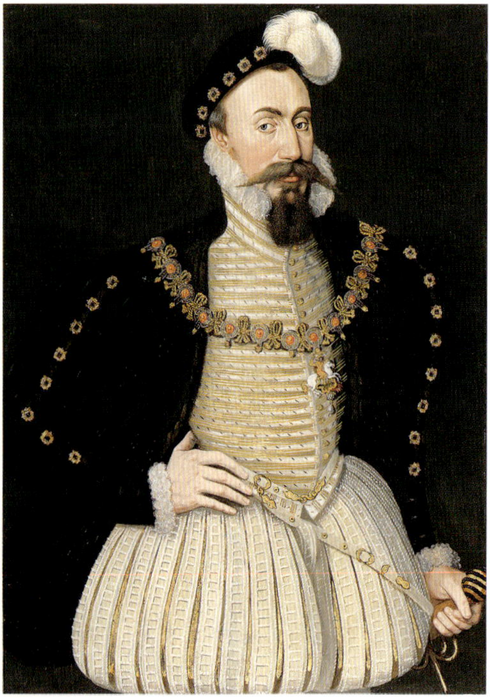

Fig. 9
ROBERT DUDLEY,
EARL OF LEICESTER
(1532?–88)
Unknown artist, *c.*1575
Oil on panel, 965 x 686mm
(38 x 27in)

The most famous and most influential of all Elizabeth I's favourites, Robert Dudley, Earl of Leicester, was the fifth son of John Dudley, Duke of Northumberland, who had briefly put his daughter-in-law Lady Jane Grey (1537–54) on the throne and subsequently been executed by Mary I. Handsome, vain and capricious, Leicester was Elizabeth's only serious English suitor during her reign. He had an uneasy relationship with her chief minister, Lord Burghley, who distrusted him and strongly opposed their marriage; Elizabeth herself found her virginity too important a political tool to abandon for his sake. Leicester was associated with a number of plots and intrigues, and rumour accused him of murdering his first wife and the former husband of his second wife (Fig. 12), but he remained the Queen's favourite from the beginning of her reign until his death. He held the lease of the former monastic lands at Montacute briefly in 1574.

The large number and great variety of surviving portraits of Leicester reflect not only his power and importance but also his intense interest in his own painted image. He evidently sat frequently to a number of different artists. In this painting, as in all his portraits, Leicester is shown dressed fashionably and expensively. He had been made a Knight of the Order of the Garter in 1559, a very high honour, and he wears the collar of the Order, with the 'Great George', a medallion depicting Saint George killing the dragon, hanging from it.

Fig. 10
SIR WALTER RALEGH
(1552?–1618)
Attributed to the
monogrammist 'H', 1588
Oil on panel, 914 x 746mm
(36 x 29 3/8 in)

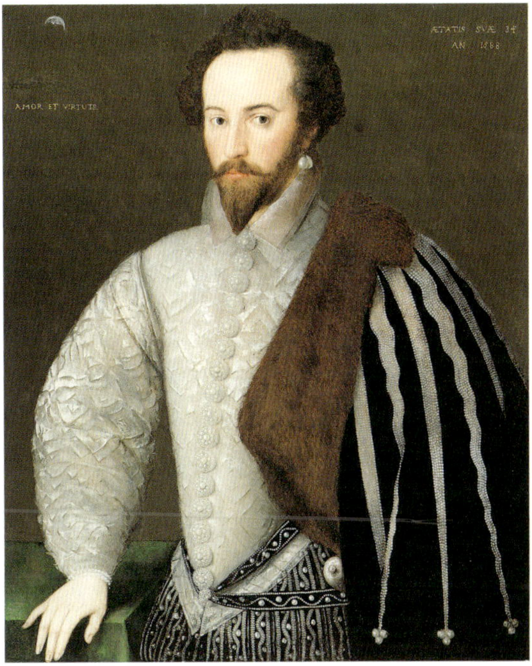

A poet, explorer, soldier, sailor, courtier and favourite of the Queen, Ralegh represented the epitome of the 'Renaissance Man' in Elizabethan England. Much of his literary work is lost, but about thirty short poems and various prose works, including *The History of the World*, survive. He organised and financed a number of expeditions to North America, but he never actually set foot there himself; in later life he made several unsuccessful attempts to find gold in South America. Alternately in and out of favour with Elizabeth, he was accused of plotting against James I, and spent much of James's reign in the Tower of London. He was eventually executed for treason in 1618.

Ralegh had a reputation for extravagant dress in his youth, and in this portrait he is shown wearing a costume lavishly embroidered with pearls. These were fashionable decoration and, as symbols of purity, may have been intended to show allegiance to Elizabeth, the 'Virgin Queen'. The pattern on Ralegh's cloak is formed by the rays of a 'sun-in-splendour', a common heraldic device used on clothing, which can also be seen on the sleeves of Elizabeth's dress in the 'Armada' portrait (Fig. 7). Like many Elizabethan paintings, Ralegh's portrait contains a mysterious symbol and an inscription which clearly had specific meanings but which are now difficult to interpret: the half-moon at the top left and the motto *Amor et Virtute* ('by love and virtue') may perhaps allude to the Queen. The picture is attributed to an artist known by his initial, 'H', by comparison with a painting in the Metropolitan Museum in New York.

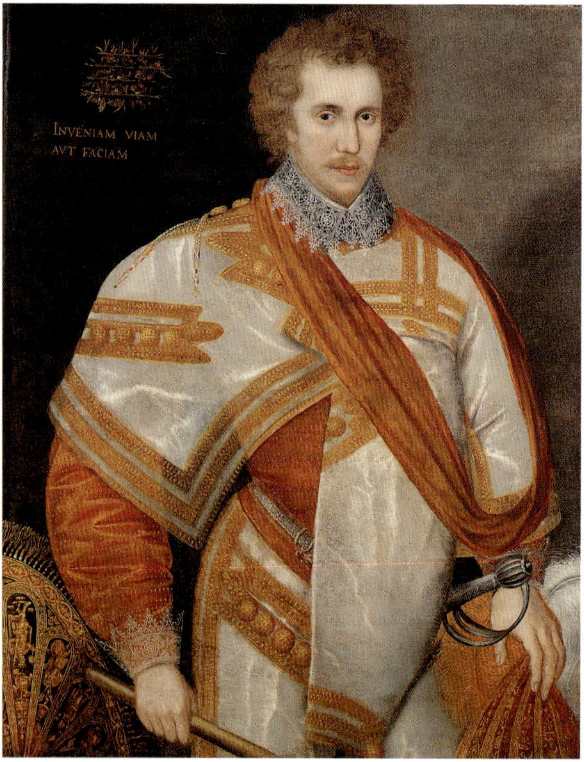

Fig. 11
ROBERT SIDNEY,
1ST EARL OF
LEICESTER
(1563–1626)
Unknown artist, *c.*1588
Oil on canvas,
991 x 794mm
(39 x 31¼ in)

The soldier brother of the poet Sir Philip Sidney (1554–86) and of Mary Sidney, Countess of Pembroke (1561–1621), Robert Sidney had a distinguished military career, particularly in the Low Countries, and he was made Governor of Flushing in 1588. He wrote poetry and was interested in music; his home life at Penshurst in Kent was described in a poem by Ben Jonson (1573?–1637). From James I he received various honours, eventually being created Earl of Leicester in 1618.

Sidney is shown in this portrait wearing a mandilion (a loose, hip-length coat) sideways over his shoulders, in a manner known as 'collie-westonward'. This was a fashion of the 1580s. The baton he holds in his right hand is a sign of military rank; his career as a soldier is also alluded to by the helmet and shield, which are Milanese. The elaborate decoration on the shield depicts Apollo as god of light and fire. In the top left-hand corner of the painting is a pictorial symbol or *impresa* of burning boughs; it is not entirely clear what meaning this symbol had for Sidney. The motto, INVENIAM VIAM AVT FACIAM, can be translated 'I shall find a way or I shall make one'.

Fig. 12
WALTER DEVEREUX,
1ST EARL OF ESSEX
(1539–76)
Unknown artist, 1575?
after a portrait of 1572
Oil on panel, 1089 x 790mm
(42 7/8 x 31 1/8 in)

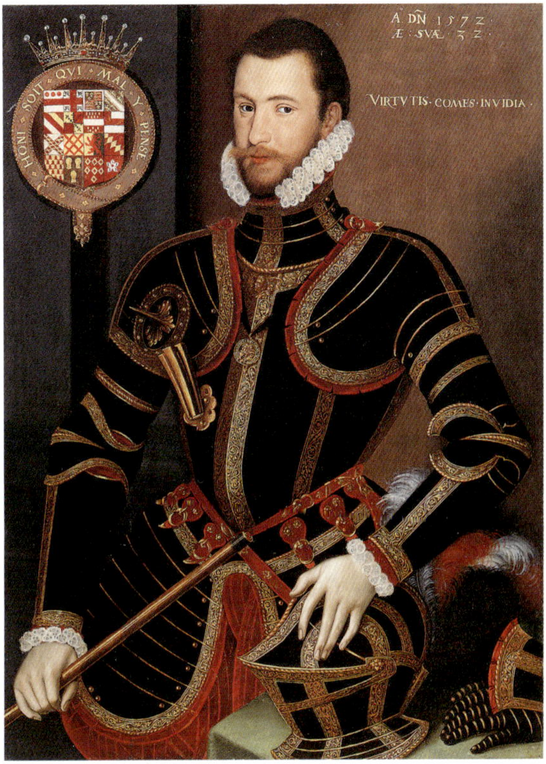

A courageous but ruthless adventurer, Walter Devereux, 1st Earl of Essex, undertook to conquer and colonise Ulster on behalf of England in 1573. After two years of brutal and treacherous dealings against the Irish and the Scots living in Ulster, during which time he lost most of his army and his money, he was recalled to England. Before he left, he carried out his most notorious act, a massacre on the island of Rathlin. Back in England, it was rumoured that his wife, Lettice, was having an affair with Queen Elizabeth's favourite, Robert Dudley, Earl of Leicester (Fig. 9). When Essex died a year after his return, gossip accused Leicester of having poisoned him; it appears, however, that he died of dysentery. Lettice married Leicester shortly afterwards. Essex was the father of Robert Devereux, the second Earl, who became the Queen's last favourite.

A number of versions of this portrait exist, of which this is one of the finest. Walter Devereux was created Earl of Essex in 1572, and also made a Knight of the Order of the Garter in that year, and a double commemoration of these two honours may have been the incentive for the production of the earliest of these paintings, all of which bear the date 1572. This particular version, however, shows Essex holding an Earl Marshal's baton; he was made Earl Marshal of Ireland in 1575, and so it seems likely that this portrait was painted at that date to celebrate the appointment. The elaborate coat of arms at the top left, surrounded by the garter and topped by an earl's coronet, reflects Essex's love of heraldry; it was said in his funeral sermon that he 'excelled in describing and blazing of arms'. Essex's arms can also be seen in one of the stained-glass windows in the library at Montacute House.

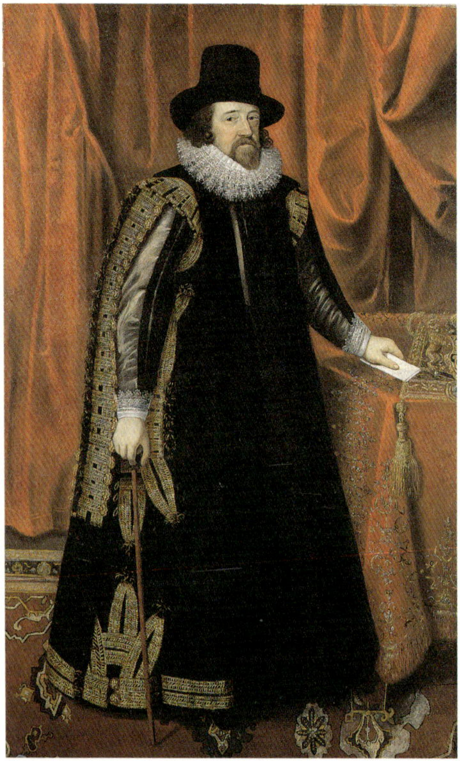

Fig. 13
FRANCIS BACON,
VISCOUNT ST ALBAN
(1561–1626)
Unknown artist, after 1731,
after a portrait of *c.*1620
Oil on canvas, 2007 x 1270mm
(79 x 50in)

A lawyer, philosopher, essayist and scientist, Francis Bacon was one of the great intellectual figures of Jacobean England. His parliamentary career peaked with his appointment as Lord Chancellor in 1618, but three years later he was impeached for bribery, confessed to 'corruption and neglect', was disgraced and imprisoned. Sir Robert Phelips of Montacute was the chairman of the committee of enquiry into the corruption charges. Bacon was soon released from prison, largely thanks to the Duke of Buckingham (Fig. 27), and, free from parliamentary distractions, he was able to bring to completion much of the philosophical and scientific work on which he had been engaged for years. He is said to have died as a result of catching cold while stuffing a chicken with snow to test the preservation of flesh by freezing, during a journey to Highgate; however, while he evidently continued making scientific experiments until the end of his life, it appears that he had been ill for some time before this famous journey took place.

Bacon is seen here in his role as Lord Chancellor, wearing parliamentary robes, with the bag containing the Great Seal on the table at the right. Almost all the existing portraits of Bacon were painted over a century after his death, although they seem to have been based on a contemporary portrait of about 1620.

Fig. 14
SIR EDWARD HOBY
(1560–1617)
Unknown artist, 1583
Oil on panel, 953 x 756mm
(37$\frac{1}{2}$ x 29$\frac{3}{4}$ in)

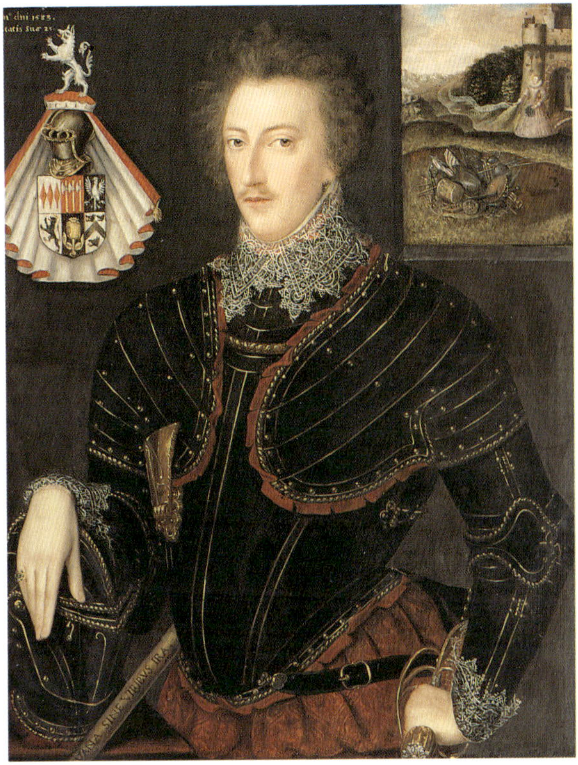

The soldier Sir Edward Hoby was, like other members of his family, also a diplomat and scholar. His father, Sir Thomas Hoby, had been an ambassador for Henry VIII. Edward Hoby was sent by Elizabeth I on a mission to Scotland in 1584, where he caught the eye of James VI; James's preference for him caused Hoby some difficulties with Elizabeth for a time, but by 1588 he was back in favour and was appointed Secretary to the Council of War that made the preparations to meet the Spanish Armada. Hoby translated a number of works from French and Spanish, and was a friend of the antiquarian Sir William Camden.

Hoby is depicted in this portrait at the age of twenty-three, wearing a suit of Greenwich armour. The baton at lower left is inscribed VANA SINE VIRIBUS IRA, meaning 'anger without strength is vain'. The mysterious inset scene at the top right shows a woman standing in front of a castle and holding a scroll or banner on which is written RECONDV̄TVR NŌ RETV̄DV̄TVR, which can be translated as 'laid aside but not blunted'. In front of the woman is a pile of discarded weapons and military trophies, covered by a veil. This scene clearly has a symbolic meaning, but it is difficult to interpret now; it may be that it refers to a temporary interruption in Hoby's military career.

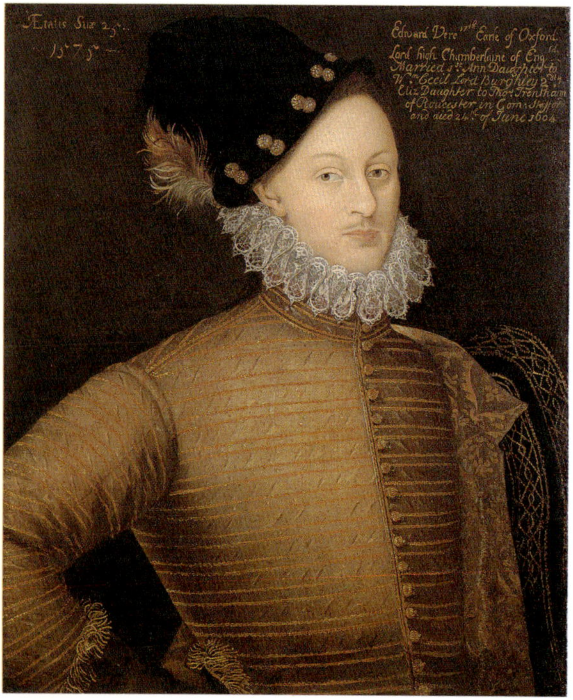

Fig. 15
EDWARD DE VERE,
17TH EARL OF OXFORD
(1550–1604)
Unknown artist, seventeenth century after a portrait of 1575
Oil on canvas, 743 x 635mm (29 1/4 x 25in)

The talented, extravagant and hot-tempered son-in-law of Lord Burghley (Fig. 8), Oxford was the hereditary Lord Great Chamberlain of England, and a favourite of Elizabeth I. He was involved in a number of dramatic quarrels with other courtiers, including Sir Philip Sidney, and he supported an expensive lifestyle by selling most of his inheritance. He was distinguished in his literary achievements, however, both as the patron of a company of actors and as an important lyric poet in his own right. It is claimed by some that he was the author of Shakespeare's plays.

No genuine contemporary portrait of Oxford is known to exist today. Stylistic evidence in this painting indicates that it is a later work, but it appears to be a copy of a portrait of 1575 that is now lost.

Fig. 16
ELIZABETH TALBOT,
COUNTESS OF SHREWSBURY
(1527–1608)
Unknown artist, probably seventeenth century after a portrait of *c.*1590
Oil on canvas, 988 x 787mm (38 7/8 x 31in)

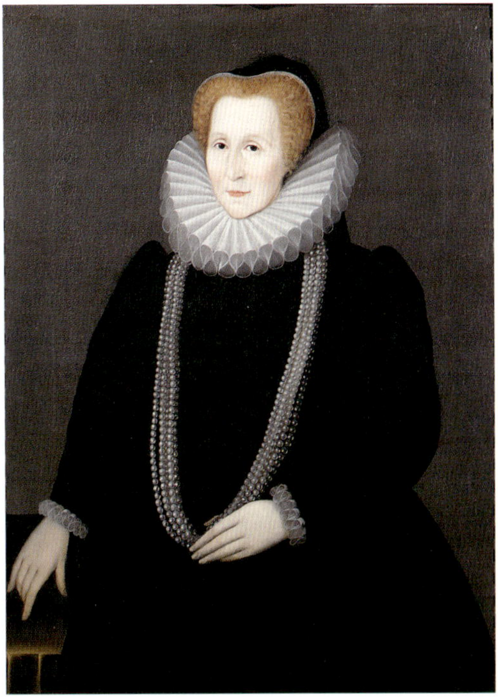

More commonly known as 'Bess of Hardwick', Elizabeth Talbot came from a family of minor gentry in Derbyshire and rose to become one of the wealthiest people in England. She married four times, to progressively more important and richer men, and throughout her life displayed extraordinary business acumen, acquisitiveness and ambition. She built a magnificent house on the land at Chatsworth which she acquired through Sir William Cavendish, her second husband, but she is remembered mainly for the house she built at Hardwick, a property she bought from her brother. After the death of her fourth husband, George Talbot, Earl of Shrewsbury (1527–90), Hardwick became her main home, and, having recently remodelled what is now known as Hardwick Old Hall, she set about building another house, the spectacular New Hall, planned almost certainly by the great Elizabethan architect Robert Smythson (*c.*1535–1614). In furnishing her homes, Bess was the patron of a great many craftsmen and women, perhaps most notably of a number of very skilful embroiderers, whose names are largely lost, but many of whose works survive at Hardwick.

This portrait shows Bess dressed as a widow, presumably after the death of her fourth husband in 1590, and is a version of a portrait at Hardwick. Although she is depicted wearing a plain dress, her wealth is clearly indicated by the enormous ropes of pearls around her neck.

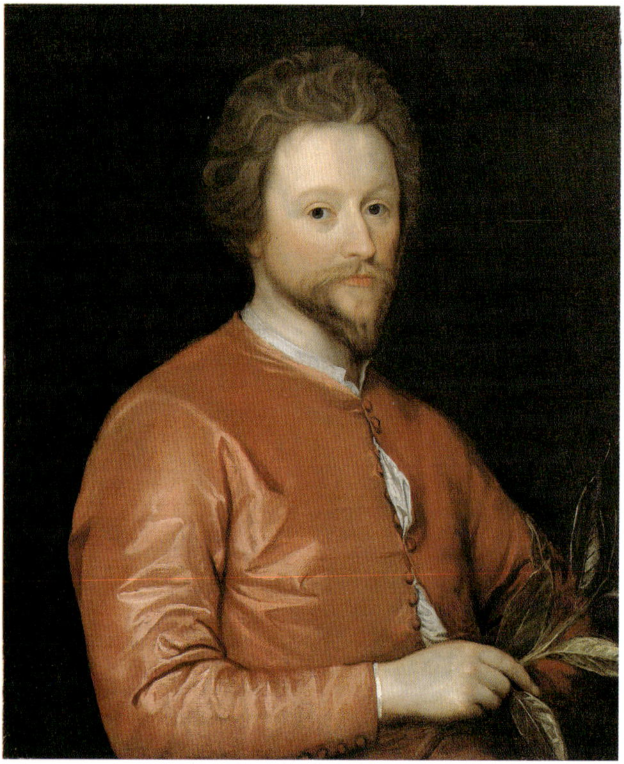

Fig. 17
JOHN FLETCHER
(1579–1625)
Unknown artist, late seventeenth century after a portrait of *c.*1620
Oil on canvas,
737 x 368mm
(29 x 14½ in)

One of the most important playwrights in Jacobean London, Fletcher is particularly known for his extremely successful collaborations with Francis Beaumont (1584–1616), including *Philaster* (*c.*1609), *The Maid's Tragedy* (*c.*1610) and *A King and No King* (1611). So successful and popular were the plays of Beaumont and Fletcher that a large number of works by other authors were ascribed to them by their contemporaries and immediate successors. In fact they may have written only seven or eight plays together. Fletcher also wrote several plays by himself, and collaborated on many works with other playwrights, including Shakespeare in *Henry VIII* and *The Two Noble Kinsmen* (both 1613). Fletcher's work had a significant influence on the development of drama in the seventeenth century.

Only one contemporary portrait of John Fletcher is known, in a private collection. The head in the present painting is copied from that portrait, but the body is a fanciful creation of the late seventeenth century. The playwright is shown holding a laurel branch, a symbol of eternity because of its evergreen properties. This symbolism implies that Fletcher has achieved immortality through his writing.

Fig. 18
SIR NATHANIEL BACON
(1585–1627)
Self-portrait, *c.*1625
Oil on panel,
feigned oval, 575 x 445mm
(22 5/8 x 17 1/2 in)

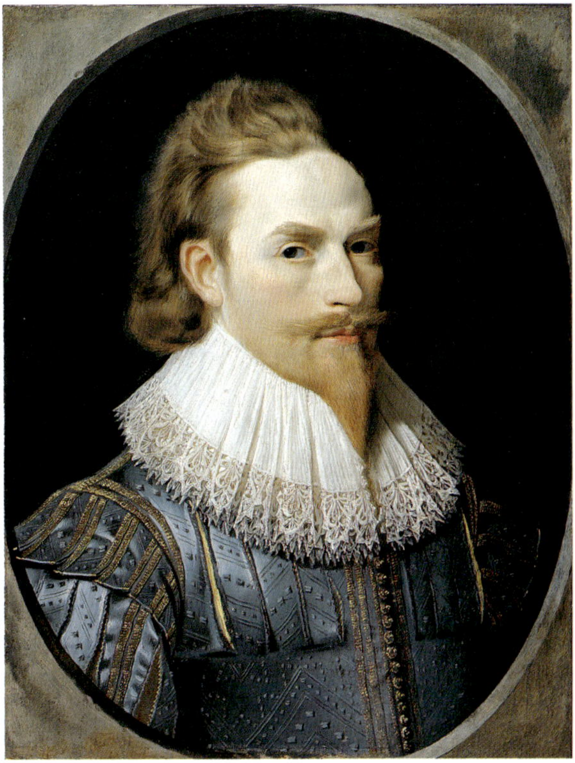

Sir Nathaniel Bacon was a wealthy landowner from East Anglia and a relation of Francis Bacon, the philosopher and scientist (Fig. 13); he was also an exceptionally skilful and innovative amateur painter. Few of his paintings survive, but the remaining works and evidence of lost paintings testify to his remarkable abilities. He was particularly known for very large market and kitchen scenes, dominated by still-life depictions of enormous vegetables and fruit, often accompanied by a buxom maid. This was a type of painting popular in the Low Countries at the time, but Bacon is the only English artist known to have worked in this genre. Surviving letters show that although he rarely travelled from his country home to London, he often visited the Netherlands, and clearly this was the source of his artistic influences.

In addition to the market scenes, a small group of self-portraits by Bacon, including this one, also bear witness to his skill as a painter. The strong contrasts between the light and dark areas and the polished refinement of the painting reflect his knowledge of Netherlandish art. The painted stone oval which surrounds the portrait is a common device in Anglo-Netherlandish portraits of this period. If it were not for the fact that we know the sitter to be Bacon by comparison with other paintings, it would be difficult to identify this as an artist's self-portrait; Bacon does not show himself as a painter but rather, with his fine satin doublet, emphasises his status as a wealthy gentleman.

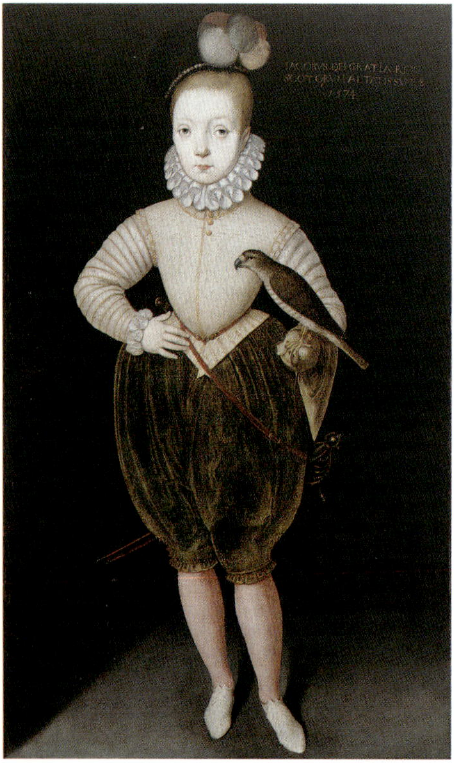

Fig. 19
JAMES VI OF SCOTLAND AND I OF ENGLAND
(1566–1625)
Attributed to Rowland Lockey after Arnold van Brounckhorst, late sixteenth century after a portrait of 1574
Oil on canvas, 1181 x 730mm
($46\frac{1}{2}$ x $28\frac{3}{4}$ in)

James was the son of Mary, Queen of Scots and her second husband Henry Stuart, Lord Darnley. His father was murdered eight months after he was born, and he saw his mother for the last time two months after that. He was crowned King of Scotland at the age of thirteen months, on the abdication of his mother, and was brought up by the Earl and Countess of Mar, in Stirling Castle. The country was run until James's majority by a succession of Protestant Regents. The young King received his education at the hands of two particularly distinguished tutors, the poet and historian George Buchanan (1506–82) and the Calvinist Peter Young (1544–1628). Intelligent and scholarly, he became an able theologian and a confirmed Protestant. He succeeded to the throne of England in 1603, and moved his court to London. A portrait of James as an adult can be seen on p.28.

This portrait of James at the age of eight shows him with a sparrowhawk on his arm; hawking was one of his favourite occupations. It is apparently based on a half-length portrait on panel in the Scottish National Portrait Gallery by Arnold van Brounckhorst (active 1565–83), who became James's official painter in 1580. James's pose in this portrait ultimately derives from one used by Hans Holbein for portraits of Henry VIII, and then adapted for Edward VI. The artist has softened its impact, compared with the portraits of James's Tudor predecessors, by placing the boy's feet relatively close together, rather than wide apart.

Fig. 20
ROBERT CAREY, 1ST EARL OF MONMOUTH (1560–1639) AND HIS FAMILY
Attributed to Paul van Somer, *c.*1617
Oil on canvas, 2273 x 2165mm (89 1/2 x 85 1/4 in)

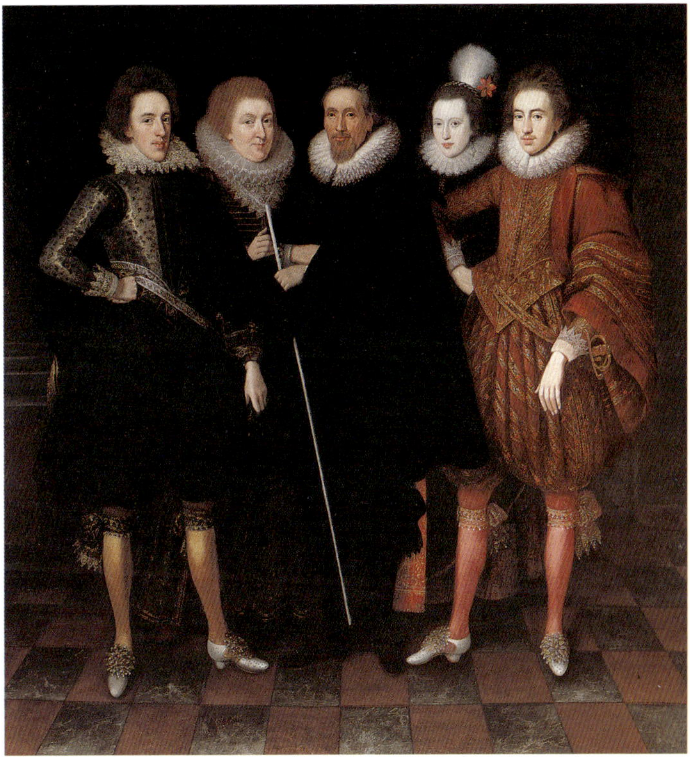

Robert Carey was a soldier and member of Elizabeth I's court. At Elizabeth's death, he tried to curry favour with James VI of Scotland by being the first to bring him the news, riding to Edinburgh from London in three days. He found employment in James's court in England, eventually rising to become Chamberlain to Prince Charles when he was created Prince of Wales in 1617. He was created Earl of Monmouth by Charles I in 1626.

Carey is seen in this portrait holding the white Chamberlain's rod, surrounded by his family. At the left are his wife, Elizabeth Trevannion (died 1641) and his elder son Henry, later the second Earl (1596–1661); at the right are his daughter Philadelphia (1594–1654), later Lady Wharton, and his younger son, Thomas (1597–1634). The artist to whom this portrait is attributed, Paul van Somer (*c.*1576–1622), was one of a number of artists from the Netherlands to arrive in England in the second decade of the seventeenth century. He quickly found favour with the royal family, and produced new portrait types of the King and Queen. Large group portraits like this one were rare in England at this date, and this painting, with its life-size figures and the row of heads framed by white ruffs and collars, is particularly dramatic.

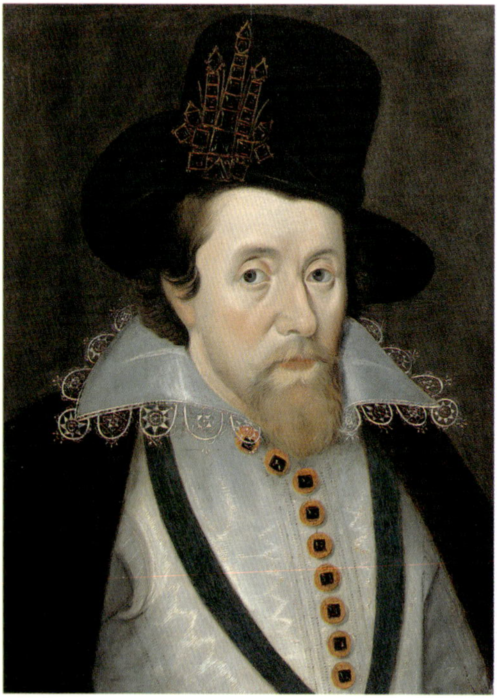

Fig. 21
JAMES VI OF SCOTLAND AND I OF ENGLAND (1566–1625)
After John de Critz the Elder, early seventeenth century after a portrait of *c.*1606
Oil on panel, 572 x 419mm (22 1/2 x 16 1/2 in)

James VI of Scotland succeeded to the throne of England in 1603, on the death of Elizabeth I, and he moved with his wife, Anne of Denmark, and three surviving children to England. James's scholarly and theological interests, the legacy of his upbringing, found expression in his adult life in a number of publications, including *Basilikon Doron* (1599), on the art of government, addressed to his elder son, Henry (Fig. 23). He also wrote *A Counterblaste to Tobacco* (1604), which refuted the popular arguments in favour of its use. James's other great interest, one which he shared with his Queen, was in hunting. He was increasingly influenced by a succession of male favourites, notably the Duke of Buckingham (Fig. 27), and this, along with his autocratic style and deep belief in the 'Divine Right of Kings', contributed to his unpopularity and the difficult political legacy he left his son, Charles I.

James disliked sitting for his portrait, and so most images of him are copies or variants of a small number of pictures painted from life. This painting is a version of the most popular portrait type of the King, produced by the artist John de Critz (*c.*1551–1642). De Critz, a painter of Flemish origin, was James's 'Serjeant Painter', with special responsibility for producing decorative paintings and portraits for the King. The portrait shows James wearing a spectacular hat jewel, one of a number of such ornaments that he owned. This jewel, called 'The Feather', was set with huge diamonds.

Fig. 22
ANNE OF DENMARK
(1574–1619)
Unknown artist after
Paul van Somer, seventeenth
century after a portrait of
*c.*1617
Oil on canvas,
feigned oval, 629 x 533mm
(24 3/4 x 21in)

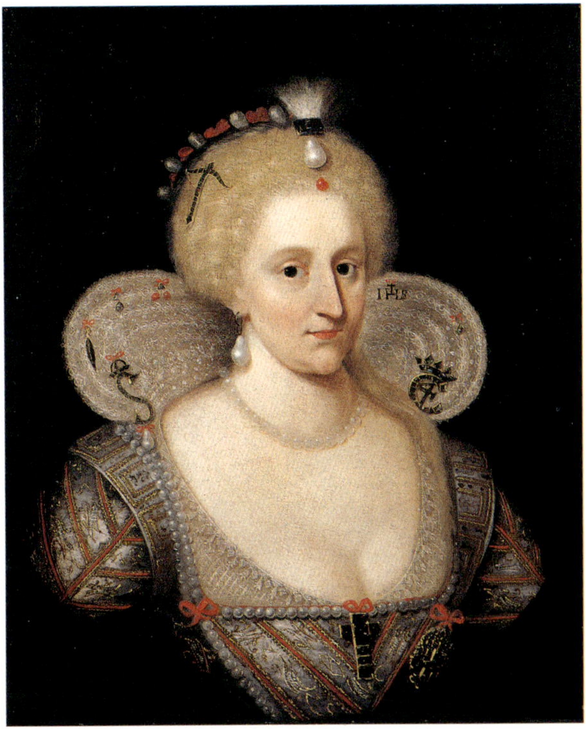

Anne of Denmark married James VI of Scotland in 1589. She gave birth to seven children, of whom three survived to adulthood: Henry, Elizabeth and Charles. On her husband's accession to the English throne in 1603, she gained more scope to indulge her interests in the arts, actively patronising poets and musicians. She is particularly remembered for commissioning great Jacobean court masques, elaborate entertainments involving acting, singing and dancing, which were performed by members of the royal family and courtiers. The most famous of these masques were collaborations between the poet Ben Jonson and the architect and designer Inigo Jones (1573–1652).

This is a version of a popular portrait type of the Queen, of which a full-length painting by Paul van Somer in the Royal Collection is probably the original. Anne is shown wearing some of the most famous and distinctive jewels from her large collection. The crossbow-shaped jewel in her hair may be one that had belonged to Elizabeth I. The crowned 'S' pinned to the left side of her collar refers to her mother, Sophia of Mecklenberg, and the crowned 'C' on the right to her brother, Christian IV of Denmark; Anne was particularly proud of her royal relations. She also wears a jewelled sacred 'IHS' monogram and a large crucifix, prominent symbols of the Catholic faith to which she had converted. The oval jewel tied with a bow is probably the case for a portrait miniature.

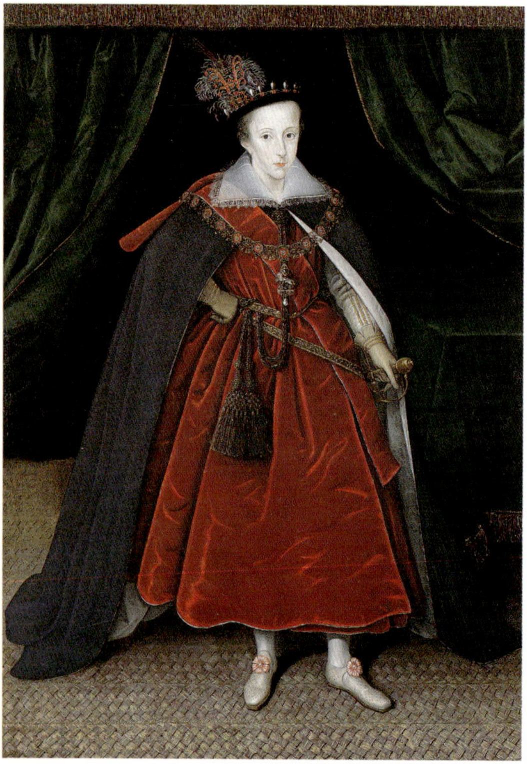

Fig. 23
HENRY, PRINCE OF WALES (1594–1612)
Attributed to Marcus Gheeraerts the Younger, *c.*1603
Oil on canvas, 1619 x 1168mm (63¾ x 46in)

Henry was the promising elder son of James VI and I and his Queen, Anne of Denmark. An ardent Protestant, enthusiastic sportsman and patron of the arts, he was regarded as England's great hope for the future. He was created Prince of Wales in 1610, but died two years later of typhoid fever. He was deeply mourned by both his own family and the public at large. Sir Edward Phelips, the builder of Montacute House, was Henry's Chancellor of the Duchy of Cornwall from 1606 until his own death in 1614.

This portrait shows Henry at about the age of nine, wearing the robes and collar of the Order of the Garter. Henry was made a Knight of the Garter on the accession of his father to the throne in 1603, and it may be that this painting was produced to commemorate that occasion. Portraits of the two Jacobean Princes, Henry and his younger brother Charles, are easily confused, and for many years this painting was thought to depict Charles (Fig. 24). On stylistic grounds, however, it can be dated to about 1603, at which date Charles was too young to be the boy shown here; moreover, Henry is recognisable by comparison with other portraits of him at about this age. The magnificent jewel in his hat, topped by a ship, can also be seen in other portraits of the young Prince.

Fig. 24
CHARLES I
(1600–49)
Attributed to Abraham
van Blyenberch, *c.*1617–20
Oil on canvas, 2007 x 1156mm
(79 x 45 1/2 in)

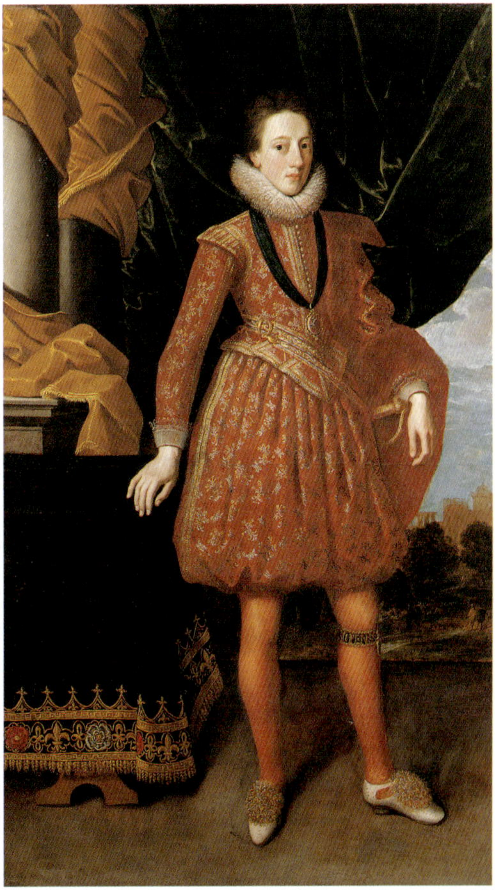

The younger, surviving son of James VI and I, Charles became heir to the thrones of England and Scotland on the death of his brother, Henry, in 1612. Like his mother and brother, he had a serious interest in the visual arts, eventually becoming the greatest of all British royal patrons and collectors. His firm belief in the Divine Right of Kings, and his high-handed dealings with Parliament, however, led to the outbreak of civil war, and he was executed in 1649.

Charles's early interest in painting is evident in this portrait, which he probably commissioned and owned himself. It is almost certainly by Abraham van Blyenberch, a Flemish artist who is recorded working in England between 1617 and 1621. It provides an interesting contrast with the portrait of his older brother Henry (Fig. 23), painted a decade and a half earlier. Like his brother, Charles is shown in an interior, with a velvet-draped table beside him and curtains behind, but van Blyenberch's painting is both more realistic and more artificial than the earlier work. The perspective of the space in which Charles stands is more fully realised, and the Prince himself has a more lifelike and animated appearance than the stiff figure of his brother. The curtains, however, sweep and fall and swathe the columns in a strikingly sculptural manner which defies gravity and logic, and the floor on which the Prince stands suddenly and irrationally gives way to a remarkably sophisticated and delicate landscape. Charles's patronage of the avant-garde van Blyenberch implies he had a remarkably sophisticated taste at a young age.

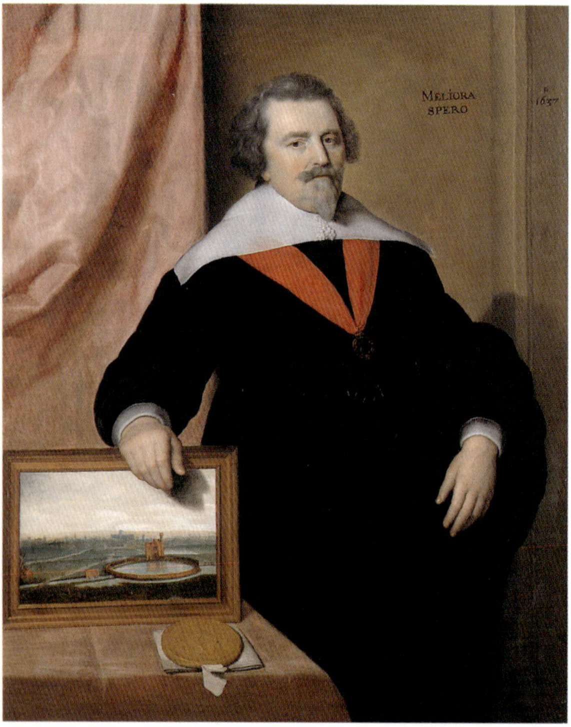

Fig. 25
SIR JOHN BACKHOUSE
(1584–1649)
By the monogrammist
'V.M.', 1637
Oil on canvas,
1283 x 1041mm
(50½ x 41in)

This very unusual portrait depicts Sir John Backhouse, a landowner and founder member of the New River Company. The Company, which received its charter in 1619 from James I, was founded to bring fresh water into London from Hertfordshire. Backhouse owned the land in Islington on which the first London reservoir was built by the Company. His pride in the project is very clearly demonstrated by the painting on which he rests his right hand; it shows the reservoir in the foreground and, behind, a view of London including the old St Paul's Cathedral. Below the painting is a folded document with a royal seal on it, presumably a copy of the charter. The motto inscribed to the right of Backhouse's head, MELIORA SPERO, is appropriate for someone involved in such a scheme of improvements, as it means 'I hope for better things'. It probably, however, refers to the rewards of Heaven rather than of this world. Backhouse wears the badge of the Order of the Bath on a ribbon around his neck, an honour bestowed on him by Charles I at his coronation.

The artist, who probably came from the Netherlands, is only known by his initials, 'V.M.'. Three other paintings by this artist are known, two of which are also dated, like this one, in the 1630s. It seems likely that the painter was only in England for a short time during that decade.

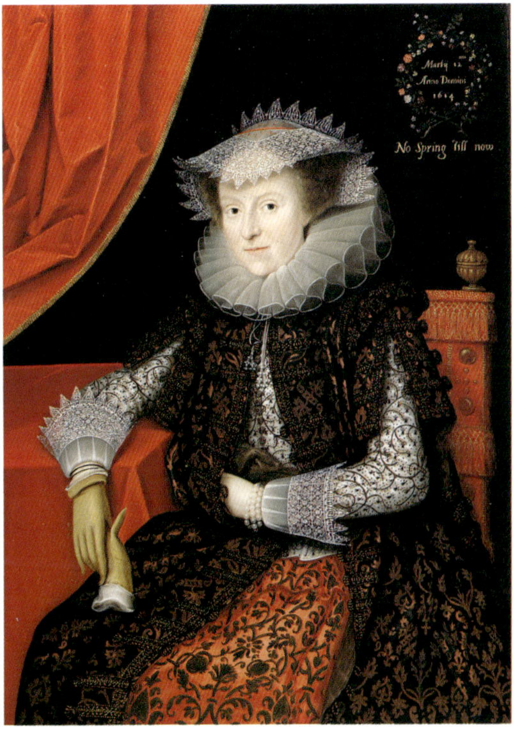

Fig. 26
MARY THROCKMORTON,
LADY SCUDAMORE
(died 1632)
Marcus Gheeraerts the Younger,
1615
Oil on panel, 1143 x 826mm
(45 x 32 1/2 in)

This beautiful portrait, one of the finest at Montacute House, was painted to commemorate the marriage of Lady Scudamore's son, John, later Viscount Scudamore, to Elizabeth Porter of Dauntsey, Wiltshire. Little is known about Lady Scudamore, but her son's marriage clearly symbolised hope and regeneration within the family; this is alluded to by the motto on the painting, 'No Spring Till now', and by the wreath of flowers surrounding the date of the marriage. At the time this portrait was painted, the New Year was calculated from 25 March, the Feast of the Annunciation, rather than from 1 January. The date of the wedding inscribed on the painting, 12 March 1614, would actually be 12 March 1615 by our calculations today.

The artist of this portrait, Marcus Gheeraerts the Younger (1561/2–1636), was one of the most important of the later Elizabethan and early Jacobean period. His family moved to London from the Netherlands when he was a child, and he came to prominence as a painter in the 1590s. The pose that he gives Lady Scudamore, with her left hand tucked into the folds of her coat, is one he used in a number of other portraits of women at about this date. What makes this painting remarkable, apart from the striking red, black and white colour scheme, is the very sensitive depiction of Lady Scudamore's thoughtful expression and her slightly melancholic half-smile.

The handsome but unscrupulous George Villiers was the most notorious of all James I's favourites. The King adored him, promoting him with astonishing rapidity through the ranks of the aristocracy. Knighted in 1615, Villiers was made a viscount, an earl and then a marquess successively over the course of three years from 1616 to 1618. Finally James made him Duke of Buckingham in 1623. He wielded enormous power over the King, and subsequently over his son Charles I, but was generally regarded with suspicion and dislike.In 1628 he was assassinated at Portsmouth.

Buckingham used much of the wealth he amassed to build up a very important art collection. He patronised the most successful and fashionable foreign artists, and, along with Charles I, was responsible for bringing the Dutch painter Gerrit van Honthorst (1590–1656) to England in 1628. Honthorst was one of the few Dutch artists of this period to gain an international reputation; he had worked in Rome and his paintings, with their dramatic lighting and smooth modelling, reflect something of the style of the much-admired Roman artist Caravaggio. This painting is a good, early copy of a portrait of the Duke and his family by Honthorst which belonged to Charles I and is still in the Royal Collection at Hampton Court. It shows Buckingham with his wife, Katherine Manners (died 1649), their daughter Mary, later Duchess of Richmond (1622–85), and their son George (1628–87), later the second Duke. It was painted very shortly before Buckingham was murdered. A second son was born posthumously.

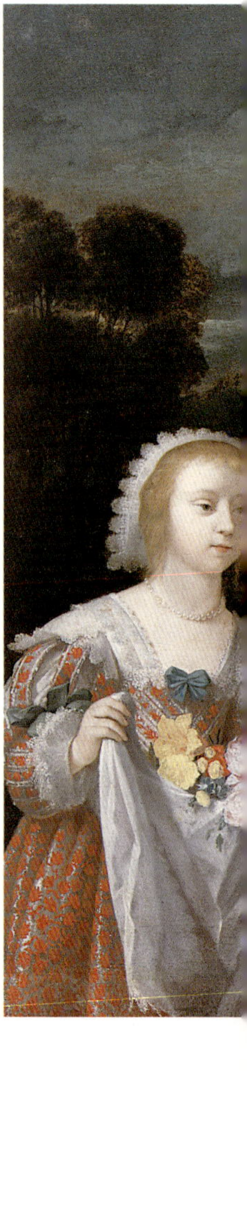

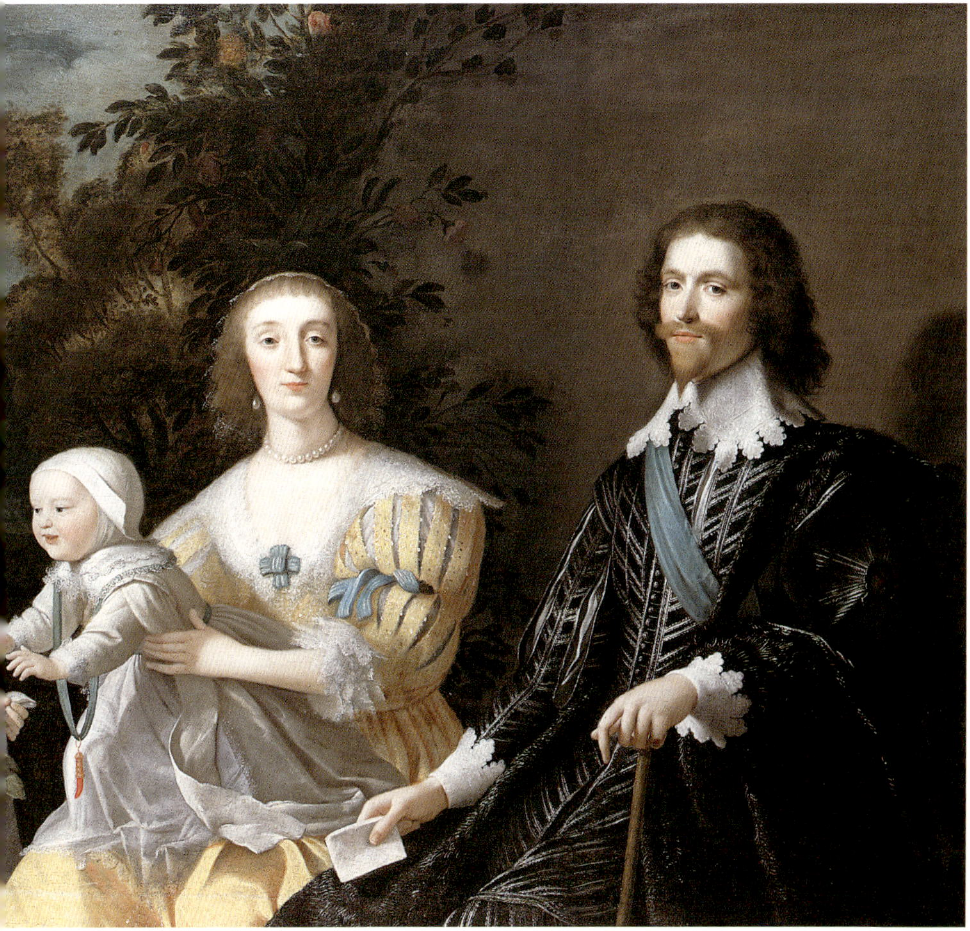

Fig. 27
GEORGE VILLIERS,
1ST DUKE OF BUCKINGHAM
(1592–1628) AND HIS FAMILY
Unknown artist after
Gerrit van Honthorst, 1628
Oil on canvas, 1454 x 1981mm
(57 1/4 x 78in)

Paintings from the National Portrait Gallery collection at Montacute House

This list is ordered alphabetically, either by title or surname, and according to the location of paintings within the house

ROOM 2

Sir William Butts (died 1545)
Unknown artist after Hans Holbein the Younger (1497 or 8–1543), sixteenth century after a portrait of *c.*1540–43
Oil on panel, 470 x 375mm (18 1/2 x 14 3/4 in)
NPG 210

Edward VI (1537–53) [Fig. 6]
Artist in the studio of William Scrots (active 1537–53), *c.*1546
Oil on panel, 473 x 279mm (18 5/8 x 11in)
NPG 442

Henry VIII (1491–1547) [Fig. 1]
Unknown artist after Hans Holbein the Younger (1497 or 8–1543), perhaps early seventeenth century after a portrait of *c.*1542
Oil on panel, 889 x 667mm (35 x 26 1/4 in)
NPG 496

Sir Thomas More (1478–1535) [Fig. 3]
Unknown artist after Hans Holbein the Younger (1497 or 8–1543), sixteenth century after a portrait of 1527
Oil on panel, 749 x 584mm (29 1/2 x 23in)
NPG 4358

Catherine Parr (1512–48) [Fig. 2]
Unknown artist, *c.*1545
Oil on panel, 635 x 508mm (25 x 20in)
NPG 4618

Sir William Petre (1505?–72) [Fig. 4]
Unknown artist, 1567
Oil on panel, 924 x 711mm (36 3/8 x 28 in)
NPG 3816

Henry Howard, Earl of Surrey (1517?–47)
Unknown artist, late sixteenth century after a portrait of 1546
Oil on panel, 419 x 286mm (16 1/2 x 11 1/4 in)
NPG 611

Sir Thomas Wyatt the Elder (1503?–42) [Fig. 5]
Unknown artist after Hans Holbein the Younger (1497 or 8–1543), sixteenth century after a portrait of *c.*1540
Oil on panel, diameter 362mm (14 1/4 in)
NPG 2809

ROOM 3

Sir Thomas Coningsby (1551–1625)
Attributed to George Gower (died 1596), 1572
Oil on panel, 940 x 699mm (37 x 27 1/2 in)
NPG 4348

Elizabeth I (1533–1603) [Fig. 7]
Attributed to George Gower (died 1596), *c.*1588
Oil on panel, 978 x 724mm (38 1/2 x 28 1/2 in)
NPG 541

Walter Devereux, 1st Earl of Essex (1539–76) [Fig. 12]
Unknown artist, 1575? after a portrait of 1572
Oil on panel, 1089 x 790mm (42 7/8 x 31 1/8 in)
NPG 4984

Robert Devereux, 2nd Earl of Essex (1566–1601)
Unknown artist after Marcus Gheeraerts the Younger (1561/2–1636), probably seventeenth century after a portrait of *c.*1596
Oil on canvas, 635 x 508mm (25 x 20in)
NPG 180

Sir Christopher Hatton (1540–91)
Unknown artist, probably seventeenth century after a portrait of 1589
Oil on panel, 781 x 654mm (30 3/4 x 25 3/4 in)
NPG 2162

Sir Edward Hoby (1560–1617) [Fig. 14]
Unknown artist, 1583
Oil on panel, 953 x 756mm (37 1/2 x 29 3/4 in)
NPG 1974

Robert Dudley, Earl of Leicester (1532?–88) [Fig. 9]
Unknown artist, *c.*1575
Oil on panel, 965 x 686mm (38 x 27 in)
NPG 247

Robert Sidney, 1st Earl of Leicester (1563–1626) [Fig. 11]
Unknown artist, *c.*1588
Oil on canvas, 991 x 794mm (39 x 31 1/4 in)
NPG 1862

Sir Walter Ralegh (1552?–1618) [Fig. 10]
Attributed to the monogrammist 'H' (active 1588), 1588
Oil on panel, 914 x 746mm (36 x 29 3/8 in)
NPG 7

Sir Nicholas Throckmorton (1515–71)
Unknown artist, *c.*1562
Oil on panel, 898 x 724mm (35 3/8 x 28 1/2 in)
NPG 3800

Sir Francis Walsingham (1530–90)
Unknown artist after John de Critz the Elder (*c.*1552–1642), sixteenth century after a portrait of *c.*1587
Oil on panel, 375 x 298mm (14 3/4 x 11 3/4 in)
NPG 1704

ROOM 4

Sir Nathaniel Bacon (1585–1627)

[Fig. 18]
Self-portrait, *c.*1625
Oil on panel, 575 x 445mm
(22 5/8 x 17 1/2 in)
NPG 2142

William Camden
(1551–1623)
Unknown artist after
Marcus Gheeraerts the
Younger (1561/2–1636),
seventeenth century
after a portrait of 1609
Oil on panel, 565 x 419mm
(22 1/4 x 16 1/2 in)
NPG 528

Thomas Sackville,
1st Earl of Dorset
(1536–1608)
Attributed to John de Critz
the Elder (*c.*1552–1642),
1601
Oil on panel, 1105 x
876mm (43 1/2 x 34 1/2 in)
NPG 4024

John Fletcher
(1579–1625)
[Fig. 17]
Unknown artist, late
seventeenth century after
a portrait of *c.*1620
Oil on canvas, 737 x 368mm
(29 x 14 1/2 in)
NPG 420

Sir John Harington
(1561–1612)
Attributed to Hieronimo
Custodis (active 1589–93),
*c.*1590–95
Oil on panel, 572 x 460mm
(22 1/2 x 18 1/8 in)
NPG 3121

Edward Herbert,
1st Baron Herbert of
Cherbury (1583–1648)
Unknown artist,
perhaps after Isaac Oliver
(*c.*1565–1617),
seventeenth century?
after a portrait of
*c.*1603–5
Oil on canvas, 737 x 610mm
(29 x 24 in)
NPG 487

Thomas Hobson
(1544?–1631)
Unknown artist, 1629
Oil on canvas, 797 x 632mm
(31 3/8 x 24 7/8 in)
NPG 1972

Ben Jonson
(1573?–1637)
Unknown artist after
Abraham van Blyenberch
(active 1617–1622),
probably early nineteenth
century after a portrait of
*c.*1617
Oil on panel, 368 x 289mm
(14 1/2 x 11 3/8 in)
NPG 363

Edward de Vere,
17th Earl of Oxford
(1550–1604)
[Fig. 15]
Unknown artist,
seventeenth century after
a portrait of 1575
Oil on canvas, 743 x 635mm
(29 1/4 x 25 in)
NPG L111 (On loan from
a private collection)

Elizabeth Talbot,
Countess of Shrewsbury
(1527–1608)
[Fig. 16]
Unknown artist, probably
seventeenth century after
a portrait of *c.*1590
Oil on canvas, 988 x 787mm
(38 7/8 x 31 in)
NPG 203

ROOM 5

Anne of Denmark
(1574–1619)
[Fig. 22]
After Paul van Somer
(*c.*1576–1622),
seventeenth century after
a portrait of *c.*1617
Oil on canvas, 629 x 533mm
(24 3/4 x 21 in)
NPG 127

Sir John Backhouse
(1584–1649)
[Fig. 25]
Monogrammist 'V.M.'
(active *c.*1637), 1637
Oil on canvas,
1283 x 1041mm
(50 1/2 x 41 in)
NPG 2183

Sir John Borlase
(1576–1648)
Michiel Jansz. van
Miereveldt (1567–1641),
1625
Oil on panel, 1130 x
911mm (44 1/2 x 35 7/8 in)
NPG 4933

George Villiers,
1st Duke of Buckingham
(1592–1628) and his
family
[Fig. 27]
Unknown artist after Gerrit
van Honthorst
(1590–1656), 1628
Oil on canvas, 1454 x
1981mm (57 1/4 x 78 in)
NPG 711

Dudley Carleton,
1st Viscount Dorchester
(1574-1632)
Michiel Jansz. van
Miereveldt (1567–1641),
*c.*1620
Oil on panel,
635 x 520mm (25 x 19 1/4 in)
NPG 3684

Sir Thomas Edmondes
(1563?–1639)
Daniel Mytens
(*c.*1590–1647), 1622
Oil on canvas, 1283 x
1016mm (50 1/2 x 40 in)
NPG 4652

Elizabeth,
Queen of Bohemia
(1596–1662)
Artist in the studio of
Michiel Jansz. van
Miereveldt (1567–1641),
*c.*1623
Oil on panel, 699 x 597mm
(27 1/2 x 23 1/2 in)
NPG 71

James VI of Scotland
and I of England
(1566–1625)
[Fig. 21]
After John de Critz the
Elder (*c.*1552–1642),
early seventeenth century
after a portrait of *c.*1606
Oil on panel, 572 x 419mm
(22 1/2 x 16 1/2 in)
NPG 548

Mary Throckmorton,
Lady Scudamore
(died 1632)
[Fig. 26]
Marcus Gheeraerts the
Younger (1561/2–1636),
1615
Oil on panel, 1143 x
826mm (45 x 32 1/2 in)
NPG 64

Horace Vere,
Baron Vere of Tilbury
(1565–1635)
Attributed to Michiel
Jansz. van Miereveldt
(1567–1641), 1629
Oil on panel, 870 x 641mm
(34 1/4 x 25 1/4 in)
NPG 818

LONG GALLERY

Francis Bacon,
Viscount St Alban
(1561–1626)
[Fig. 13]
Unknown artist, after
1731, after a portrait
of *c.*1620
Oil on canvas, 2007 x
1270mm
(79 x 50 in)
NPG 1288

?Lucy Harington,
Countess of Bedford
(1581–1627)
Unknown artist, *c.*1603
Oil on canvas, 1914 x
1138mm
(75 3/4 x 44 3/4 in)
NPG 5688

William Cecil,
1st Baron Burghley
(1520–98)
[Fig. 8]
Unknown artist, 1590s
Oil on canvas, 2230 x
1403mm
(88 1/4 x 55 1/4 in)
NPG 4881

James Hay, 1st Earl
of Carlisle (died 1636)
Unknown artist, 1628
Oil on canvas, 1946 x
1200mm
(76 5/8 x 47 1/4 in)
NPG 5210

Charles I (1600–1649) [Fig. 24]
Attributed to Abraham van Blyenberch (active 1617–22), *c.*1617–20
Oil on canvas, 2007 x 1156mm
(79 x 45 1/2 in)
NPG 1112

Robert Devereux, 3rd Earl of Essex (1591–1646)
Unknown artist, *c.*1620
Oil on canvas, 2032 x 1219mm
(80 x 48 in)
NPG L115 (On loan from a private collection)

Henry, Prince of Wales (1594–1612) [Fig. 23]
Attributed to Marcus Gheeraerts the Younger (1561/2–1636), *c.*1603
Oil on canvas, 1619 x 1168mm
(63 3/4 x 46 in)
NPG 2562

James VI of Scotland and I of England (1566–1625) [Fig. 19]
Attributed to Rowland Lockey (active 1592–1616) after Arnold van Brounckhorst (active *c.*1565–83), late sixteenth century after a portrait of 1574
Oil on canvas, 1181 x 730mm
(46 1/2 x 28 3/4 in)
NPG 63

Robert Carey, 1st Earl of Monmouth (1560–1639) and his family [Fig. 20]
Attributed to Paul van Somer (*c.*1576–1622), *c.*1617
Oil on canvas, 2273 x 2165mm (89 1/2 x 85 1/4 in)
NPG 5246

Philip Herbert, 4th Earl of Pembroke (1584–1650)
Unknown artist, *c.*1615
Oil on canvas, 2275 x 1419mm
(89 5/8 x 55 7/8 in)
NPG 5187

Lodovick Stuart, 1st Duke of Richmond and Lennox (1574–1624)
Paul van Somer (*c.*1576–1622), *c.*1620
Oil on canvas, 2077 x 1213mm
(81 3/4 x 47 3/4 in)
NPG 5297

John Thornborough (1551–1641)
Unknown artist, 1630
Oil on canvas, 2032 x 1235mm
(80 x 48 5/8 in)
NPG 5234

TRANSEPTS

Anne Boleyn (1507–36)
Unknown artist, late sixteenth century?
Oil on panel, 565 x 435mm
(22 1/4 x 17 in)
NPG 4980(15)

Edward III (1312–77)
Unknown artist, late sixteenth century?
Oil on panel, 582 x 447mm
(23 x 17 1/2 in)
NPG 4980(7)

Edward IV (1442–83)
Unknown artist, late sixteenth century?
Oil on panel, 573 x 448mm
(22 1/2 x 17 1/2 in)
NPG 4980(10)

Edward V (1470–83)
Unknown artist, late sixteenth century?
Oil on panel, 580 x 445mm
(22 4/5 x 17 1/2 in)
NPG 4980(11)

Henry I (1068–1135)
Unknown artist, *c.*1620
Oil on panel, 580 x 440mm
(22 4/5 x 17 1/3 in)
NPG 4980(2)

Henry II (1133–89)
Unknown artist, *c.*1620
Oil on panel, 558 x 413mm
(22 x 16 1/4 in)
NPG 4980(4)

Henry III (inscribed EDVARDVS) (1207–72)
Unknown artist, *c.*1620
Oil on panel, 579 x 450mm
(22 4/5 x 17 2/3 in)
NPG 4980(6)

Henry IV (1367–1413)
Unknown artist, late sixteenth century?
Oil on panel, 580 x 445mm
(22 4/5 x 17 1/2 in)
NPG 4980(9)

Henry VII (1457–1509)
Unknown artist, late sixteenth century
Oil on panel, 570 x 445mm
(22 1/2 x 17 1/2 in)
NPG 4980(13)

Henry VIII (1491–1547)
Unknown artist, late sixteenth century
Oil on panel, 582 x 450mm
(23 x 17 2/3 in)
NPG 4980(14)

John (1167?–1216)
Unknown artist, *c.*1620
Oil on panel, 575 x 450mm
(22 2/3 x 17 2/3 in)
NPG 4980(5)

Mary I (1516–58)
Unknown artist, late sixteenth century
Oil on panel, 574 x 448mm
(22 1/2 x 17 1/2 in)
NPG 4980(16)

Richard II (1367–1400)
Unknown artist, late sixteenth century?
Oil on panel, 578 x 443mm
(22 4/5 x 17 1/2 in)
NPG 4980(8)

Richard III (1452–85)
Unknown artist, late sixteenth century
Oil on panel, 567 x 447mm
(22 1/2 x 17 1/2 in)
NPG 4980(12)

Stephen (1097?–1154)
Unknown artist, *c.*1620
Oil on panel, 580 x 448mm
(22 4/5 x 17 2/3 in)
NPG 4980(3)

William I (1027–87)
Unknown artist, *c.*1620
Oil on panel, 570 x 415mm
(22 1/2 x 16 1/3 in)
NPG 4980(1)

Fig. 2 was acquired with the help of the National Art Collections Fund and the Pilgrim Trust.

Published by National Portrait Gallery Publications
National Portrait Gallery
St Martin's Place
London WC2H 0HE
www.npg.org.uk/publications

Reprinted 2002

ISBN 1-85514-278-3

Written by Catharine MacLeod
Project Manager Alison Effeny
Printed by Grillford Limited

Front cover shows:
ROBERT CAREY, 1ST EARL OF MONMOUTH,
AND HIS FAMILY
Attributed to Paul van Somer, *c.*1617
Oil on canvas

NATIONAL
PORTRAIT
GALLERY

National Portrait Gallery
St Martin's Place
London WC2H 0HE

Telephone: 020 7306 0055
Fax: 020 7306 0056
www.npg.org.uk

Montacute House
Montacute
Somerset TA15 6XP

Telephone: 01935 823 289
Fax: 01935 823289
www.nationaltrust.org.uk